THE MOON
MY LOVER
MY MOTHER
& THE DOG

THE MOON
MY LOVER
MY MOTHER
& THE DOG

poems by
Daniel McGinn

~ 2018 ~

The Moon, My Lover, My Mother, & the Dog
© Copyright 2018 Daniel McGinn
All rights reserved. No part of this book may be used or reproduced in any manner whatsoever without written permission from either the author or the publisher, except in the case of credited epigraphs or brief quotations embedded in articles or reviews.

Editor-in-chief:
Eric Morago

Associate Editors:
Michael Miller
Danielle Mitchell

Proofreader:
Jim Hoggatt

Front cover design:
Michael McGinn

Book & back cover design:
Michael Wada

Author photo:
Lori McGinn

Moon Tide logo design:
Abraham Gomez

The Moon, My Lover, My Mother, & the Dog
is published by Moon Tide Press

Moon Tide Press #166
6745 Washington Ave., Whittier, CA 90601
www.moontidepress.com

FIRST EDITION

Printed in the United States of America

ISBN # 978-0-9974837-3-4

*For my children
Michael, Dylan, and Bonnie*

CONTENTS

Foreword by Brendan Constantine	9
The Flame	13
Now That I'm Sixty	14
Phonophobia	15
The Chair	16
Eddie	17
The Next Morning	18
The Bones	19
A Letter From Maui	20
Beatles or Beach Boys? That is the Question	22
Keef	23
The Mist	24
The Grinder	25
Ferlinghetti Clouds	26
Ghost Moon	27
The Passenger	29
The Mountain	30
Teach a Man to Fish	31
Let's Live a Long Time	32
Poem 49	33
Mother Laughing	34
The Memorial	35
There Are 27 Objects Hidden in This Poem	36
The Passenger	37
Night in Transit	38
The One About the Bathtub	40
For the Birds	41
Coyote Moon	42
I'm Sure I Want to Do This	44
Ken	45
Note to Self	46
For the Attendant Who Changes Me	47
The Ghost	49
The Dead	50
Mother	51
Balloon Moon	52
Poodle Nurse	53
This is Not a Pipe Moon	54

Mother Losing Her Mind	55
My Wife Talks to Strangers	56
April	57
Alzheimer's Yard	60
Visiting Mother	61
Junkyard Moon	62
The Blight	63
Strawberries in Spring	64
I Am Ready to Listen When You Are Ready to Talk	65
Outside	66
Baby Picture	67
What I Want	68
Flower Child	69
We Called it the Bright Spot	71
Infidel	72
American Moon	73
Death in the Village	74
The First Time	75
The Passenger	76
Blood Moon	77
The Dark	78
His Marbles	80
You Are My Sunshine	81
Running Away From Home	82
A Woman Can't Hold All the Storm in Her Head	83
The Passenger	84
Everybody Knows a Wolf Can't Smile	85
Grace	86
Church	87
The Altar Boy	88
The Sandbox	89
About the Author	91
Acknowledgements	92

FOREWORD

I first became aware of Daniel McGinn at a poetry reading in 1995. At the time, he was part of a local, coffee-house scene of writers in Orange County, California and regarded as a comparative latecomer. This sense of lateness was ironic considering most of the area's 'established' voices were pushing twenty-something, making McGinn an elder statesman at nearly forty. He was also married with children big enough to headline at the same coffee house. But, during his introduction, the host emphasized twice that McGinn hadn't been writing very long. I remember being perplexed by all the disclaimers, the spoken ones and the general vibe of "He's green but he's ours!" What made it even more confusing was McGinn's brilliance. This was a fully formed poet, at once vivid and restrained. So, what made him new? Or rather, what made him late?

Fran Lebowitz once noted that when it comes to writing, there are no child prodigies as one finds in music. Mozart, we're told, could play the harpsichord at age six. A writer however, must have not only talent but a store of experiences. The more the better (Hell, the worse the better). There can be no baby Mozarts at *our* keyboards. If you ask me, there's no such thing as a latecomer; the moment you start to write is always the right moment.

It's been over twenty years since that first encounter. Daniel McGinn has since picked up a degree, published extensively, and generally embodied the life of the modern poet. This latest book, the one you're holding right now, represents his second full length effort. It's a thrilling collection, one I have truly enjoyed reading and re-reading. It's also provoked the questions I asked at the top of this introduction. Indeed, something about these poems put me smack in the middle of 1995 and I just figured out what it is. They feel young.

That is, they read like the work of someone newly drunk on poetry, someone trying out new magic. McGinn's is exciting precisely because he has preserved the fearlessness of a younger poet while writing with exquisite craft and discretion. He seems at the height of his powers here. And here the world is adored, laughed at, danced about and mourned in poems at once urgent and elegant. "Sing to me," he says, "be straight with me, tell me who you really are / and I will cling to every word like moss, like a baby, / like a leech…"

Brendan Constantine
Los Angeles, 2017

All poems are found poems
—William Stafford

THE FLAME

I don't know what to write about I tell her
Write about how you feel she says
But I don't know how I feel I tell her
I don't know how to talk about feelings
You walk around all day talking to yourself
and you tell me how you feel all the time she says
I was hoping to talk to the reader
like you and I talk to each other I tell her
but poetry is a strange way to talk I think
It's like inviting a guest into your daydreams
I was hoping to write a normal book I say
a book that normal people would want to read
Just follow the light she says
the light is free to go wherever it wants she says
as she goes to the candle she keeps on the table
and lights its brittle wick

NOW THAT I'M SIXTY

I can learn to say I'm sorry
I would rather dance with you than run from you

Look at me
Look at these things I still have to do

Children are more than background noise
Children are like the ocean

Let the neighbors run off to work
I'm happy I never killed anybody

I spill my guts to the ripe red tomatoes
Every time a mother dies all the babies cry

Children are more than mirrors
Children are more than anything

Sweet-talk the white flowers
Marvel at the strawberries

Children are more than an echo
Every little thing makes ripples

PHONOPHOBIA

Have you seen the way children play? They will talk
to a stick as if it were a man. They speak life into the air
around them. They drag everything out and leave it on
the lawn. They tear things into pieces. They dress dolls
for dinner parties. They break what needs to be broken.
They cluster in packs like wild dogs. They are not like me,
they don't take no for an answer.

Sometimes my house becomes a playground, floors shake
with running children; I cannot stop gathering information,
even as I sleep. A game show is yelling from the television,
there is laughter in the hallway, the toilet flushes and I hear
water pushing through the pipes. My ears work like hands,
cupping the unseen, again and again. I hear young, busy,
full of nonsense voices echo the impossibility of death.

I wish someone would have warned me about old age,
how the sound of all those years come seeping through
the walls. I've reached the limit of what ears can hold.
Everything contains an echo, even my own voice, resting
on my tongue like a breath mint, sweet until I swallow
and it burns on the way down.

When noise stops my ears begin to ring. The sounds
that circled around start to overflow, like a clogged drain,
all the things I've heard begin to back up and words spill out
into the air around me. I would tell the voices filling my head
that they have to leave now but I know the truth. I'm the one
who needs to go.

THE CHAIR

Another poet's chair is empty
like the clothing the poet used to wear
and the place at the table where John
and Ed and Cat and Jack once sat.

It's beginning to happen to poets
I've known for years. We grow old
and we start shrinking, malignant
cells betray us, enlarged hearts stop,
exhausted kidneys fail, lungs exhale
for one last time and then my friends
are gone.

I'm writing to you from my quiet room,
surrounded by bookcases full of poetry
books and books of essays on the craft.
No one will want to read these books
any more than they will want to sit
in a dead man's chair.

I'm getting to the age where I know
I should clear them out, so no one
needs to box my books and take them
to the thrift store when I die. I tried.
It's easy to get rid of novels but I can't
let go of poetry, not yet. These books
echo where I was and what I was writing
when I acquired them; at least half
are signed and inscribed by poets I love.

Walk into my library after I die,
you will be surrounded by my books,
little houses for the voices of my friends,
some of them are dead; none of them
were silenced.

EDDIE

Your breathing is harder now, I can see the death suit, your skeleton has begun to emerge from your skin, you keep coming back to life when someone enters the room, voices wake you, everything you say is the last thing, always a craftsman, leaving nothing unresolved, choosing the right tool and putting it back where it belongs.

You lean forward in your chair like you're about to stand up, Joanne asks *are you going somewhere?* You reply *I think so, but I can't be certain.*

THE NEXT MORNING

I'm sitting next to the smell of your ashtray full of smoked butts remembering how you tasted when you kissed me goodbye. I didn't inhale but your kiss reminded me that your insides are full of smoke, or is it ash? And I remember you saying you saw the doctor because your lungs hurt like something had crawled into the blank space behind your ribcage and fallen asleep. How heavy the sleep of ashes must be.

THE BONES

The bones in me are not the bones in the earth
The bones in me struggle with silence
The bones in me argue with the dead
As I live and breathe things must change
The dead are jealous of nothing

A LETTER FROM MAUI

I woke up this morning with the birds. The doves
began cooing just before the sun came up over the volcano.
We slept with the sliding glass door open to allow in the breeze.
The beach is right across the street.

I warm the teakettle on a tiny stove and make a cup of coffee—
fresh ground dark roast in a drip cone—and listen
as one bird after another joins the sunrise chorus.
I wish you could be here to hear it.

I make breakfast while trying not to wake Lori.
Sometimes I slice apple bananas, pineapple and mangos
and eat them from a cereal bowl with banana bread on the side.

Today I cut a papaya in half, scooped out the seeds
and drizzled it with lime juice. There are papayas growing
in arms reach of our front door. I like it here, on the second floor,
with the papayas and the birds. A rooster just crowed, alerting me
that the chickens are awake and pecking seeds in our parking lot.

It's a quarter mile to my favorite stretch of beach.
I pass fruit stands by the side of the road and the fish taco truck
where we get shrimp over rice with capers and garlic.
I always double-check the church parking lot
to see if the guy is setting up barbeque pits.

It only happens once or twice a week but when it does
we always buy a rotisserie chicken basted in hula-hula sauce.
Lori and I never finish a whole chicken
and our dog isn't here to help us
so for the first time in my life I started making chicken salad.
I didn't know I liked chicken salad.

Dressed in shorts, a light shirt and flip-flops,
I leave Lori sleeping in the tropical breeze
that fills our studio apartment.

I head for the beach. I walk in the sand
and then I walk in the water. I do this every day.
I walk until I forget I'm walking. I talk to myself
until I stop talking and I notice things.

The shadow of a crane as it flies overhead,
morning clouds, breaking waves, broken coral
washed ashore with sea glass, my own footprints,
a ghost crab scuttling back to its hole,
myna birds and cardinals landing in the trees,
those beautiful trees…

BEATLES OR BEACH BOYS?
THAT IS THE QUESTION

My grandson and I are listening to *Pet Sounds*, Gavin's favorite
CD by The Beach Boys. It's the one where Brian Wilson sits alone
in his room singing about how God only knows what he'd be
without her. I've always wondered if he ever had her.
The Beach Boys sang songs about watching girls from a distance.
Wouldn't it be nice?

We are on our way to Huntington Beach and Gavin is disappointed
we didn't get there when the sun was coming up because the sun
is the planet that controls the waves and when the sun is closer
to the ocean the waves are bigger. Everybody knows that.

Gavin's ten years old and we get into a heated discussion about
who was the best band ever? It comes down to The Beatles or
The Beach Boys. I try to explain to him that The Beatles sang to girls,
and the girls understood that they weren't afraid to talk to them
and everybody could see that it was a short distance between
I want to hold your hand and
when I touch you I feel happy, inside…

There's only so much I can explain to him—he's still a kid—
I don't think we're ready to have that talk about the Rolling Stones,
or about how quickly life is going to change. I do need to tell him
that life is about balance. For every Lennon, there's a McCartney.

We all fall in love, get acquainted with sorrow and yearn for yesterday
but seriously, how do you sleep when you're crippled inside? I don't know,
maybe we should ask Brian Wilson.

Gavin and I are just like everybody else, looking for our place on the tree.
I'm 63 and we both wish we were grown-ups.

KEEF

Keith Richards rolled a five-pound note and snorted a sample of his father's ashes cut with a line of pharmaceutical-grade cocaine. His father tasted bitter but he burned like a Viking ship, inflaming the nasal passage, causing Keith to bleed a bit of English blood, maybe just a drop or two on a cocktail napkin as he bowed his head to the bar and allowed his father's ghost to expand like a cloud in the otherwise hard blue sky.

THE MIST

I was a boy watching a cloud come down
to nest in the leaves of a grove of orange trees
where I walked and my sidewalk sneakers
never stepped on a crack in the suburban town
where it never snowed and it seldom rained.

I would spit on the ground to prove I was a boy
and launch great gusts of breath
from the window of my mouth
to watch the whiteness burst from my lungs
like a miniature cloud and if there was a glass—
a backseat window, a storefront reflection—
I would fog it up and write
the letters of my name in a patch of mist
and never look back to watch myself disappear.

The morning my mother chose to leave I watched her
descend in a cloud that covered the snow and trees
on the slope of a mountain. I watched from a window
of a building in a valley as a flock of birds winged by.
I don't know what kind of birds they were
but their timing was terrific.

I saw her again today when I looked out the curtains
from the 36th floor I saw the marine layer that hovered
over Elliot Bay begin to drift towards me. My mother
was there, in that particulate, looking to cling
to anything green. Before she evaporated I saw her bead up
and fall in streaks on the other side of the window glass
in a hotel room where I happened to be passing through.

THE GRINDER

Here is my song   bolted to a concrete floor   the music is gray   a chainsaw ripping   a howl in the fog   a tree stripped of leaves   stacked into cords   I put plugs in my ears   I am one with the machine   until death do us part   flecks flung from paper   seeps out of cracks   like a swarm of gnats   dust circles my nostrils   see how it drifts   and nests in my lungs   like gusts of snow   that cling to roof beams

I tighten the tolerance   of knives   and make the grinder   sink its teeth deep into the spines   of forgotten books   medical records   court depositions   studio scripts   photos of school children   everything ripped to shreds   tossed like confetti   pressed by a plunger   forced into bales   by this machine   that pressed a bloody towel   against my leg   and pushed me   out the door

FERLINGHETTI CLOUDS

Herds sail across the blue sea
without enough sense to rain. They huddle,
drift and return to vapor. Exhausted
buses breathe blue breath, leaving trails of smoke
as they rumble up alongside me.
Sunlight glints from chrome ribs to blind my eyes.
Faces in the windows stare out.
I shield my forehead and wait for them to leave.
This is not my bus. I am waiting for my bus
to take me away. I am lonely on a blue bench
below forgotten telephone wires.
Hydraulic doors wheeze open and shut. I return
to my book and try to read. I am not ready
to hear this and can't understand the sentences
that drift by me like the homeless—hungry
for some kind of context—shuffling feet
down the long street which is, of course,
the street of the world.

GHOST MOON

Lori said tonight's moon is a ghost moon.
I don't know what's true; sometimes Lori just makes shit up.
Lori lit a candle and put it on the back of a paper crane.
She placed it in the water and whispered a name.
Lori may be wrong sometimes
but she tells me she has the one true faith.
She makes me nervous and I forget my manners.
I didn't even think to ask if her faith was placed
on the paper crane, the lit flame or the ghost moon.
It is an old moon. I saw it late this afternoon.
The sun was up and the moon was up too.
It kept staring at me, sulky and silent.
I could see right through its skin.
It gave me the creeps.
That ghost moon followed me all the way
to the airport. It tried to hide behind a tree.
I saw it out of the corner of my eye
when I checked my bags, curbside.
I turned to look at its face
and it disappeared.
I felt a cold wind blowing up my spine.
I stood in yellow footprints
and crossed my wrists above my head.
I don't know what these machines
are supposed to do about terror
but they helped me escape the moon willies.
I walked to the gate
where I sat in a chair by a window
and thought about Lori and her paper crane.
The moon pressed its face against the glass.
It looked hungry. It had lost a lot of weight.
I walked the bridge from the terminal
and entered the aircraft.
I put my bag in an overhead compartment.
The stewards put on a show
about what to do when the jet crashes.
They performed right there in the aisle
with props and visual aids.

I was sick to death of dramatics.
I began to fear the shape of the theater I was sitting in.
My head dropped to one side and I was listening.
Turbines were spinning.
I dreamt I was spinning inside of a bullet.
The captain came on the loudspeaker
and asked us to fasten our seat belts.
We began to plummet down the runway.
My legs started shaking like a puppet.
I was strapped to a gurney in a throbbing pulse of a room.
When the turbines hit a high falsetto, we were launched into the sky.
I opened the plastic window shade
and the moon was still out there and it was watching me.
I looked down at the bay.
There were ghosts hidden in the white caps.
I saw ghosts swimming in the water.
Lori says that, in Korea, ghosts always occupy bodies of water.
New York City ghosts bump elbows with people.
They look you in the eye as they rob you of your sleep.
These ghosts must be from out of town.
I saw them out there, bathed in special light.
They swam like jellyfish in thin silk sheets.
I wondered if these ghosts had ever been dead.
I saw their wings unfold they reminded me of Lori.
When the ghosts began to burn I spoke her name out loud.

THE PASSENGER

When my father divorced us, he bought himself a muscle car, a Grand Prix. This is when the roads were new and freshly paved, when a man could ignore the seatbelts and brown-bag a beer. The moon was brighter then, the street lights fewer. It's late at night and my father is laughing, he chain smokes with windows rolled up, a cigarette smolders in the ashtray and another hangs loose from his lower lip. I'm happy to be with my dad. He smells like hair tonic, stale liquor and cigarette smoke, three things I attach to manhood. He is teaching me about blackjack, about how a player, and a dealer, each hit streaks in life. *When you are losing*, my father tells me, *don't put down more than the minimum it takes to stay in the game, that's important. Every time you win two hands in a row, double your bet. Play your cards right, I do and that's how I got this fine automobile*, he says to me, grinning.

THE MOUNTAIN

I couldn't see anything but the road in front of me and windshield wipers opening and closing their watery eyes. I was looking through a gap at the bottom of my windshield. The defroster was weak and I'd pushed it past the limit. An SUV blinded me behind a wave that curled off its back tires and I couldn't brake without chancing a fishtail so I let off the gas and slowed to a near stop as the water came down in a blanket that covered my clouded window. I slowed down but couldn't find the side of the road. I crawled forward like a cripple and used the sleeve of my jacket like a rag. I cussed and smudged-up the inside of my window in hard circles like I'd smudged-up my life and I felt older than this beat-up truck, which was all I could afford.

TEACH A MAN TO FISH

Here a thin silver line tied with a bow
to a lead weight shaped like a tear drop
dropped with a plunk in the ocean.
Sadness ripples in my ribs. I don't know why
there is an ocean in my chest or how
I'm supposed to carry it without spilling it
out all over the place. I want to shut down
for days. I want you to understand
when I disappear in the blue, silver and lead.
I have a primitive heart. I breathe underwater.
I am a wave going forward
but the ocean keeps calling me back.
Dragged like a prisoner, I have no choice
but to do this thing, to curl up in the water,
to turn in my sleeplessness, I can remain
down here for a long, long time.

LET'S LIVE A LONG TIME

So everyone will see how much I tremble
when you take my hand.

Let's die in our beds.
My shadow will never leave you.

It will lie down on your body
and start living on your bones.

POEM 49

You are wind blowing between lives
You move green leaves

You surprise me
like seeds surprise earth

You are pretty as 29 gardens
that rise and fall in the sun and rain

You hold my arm
like a leaf holds a branch

Out shadows stand in a long field
gazing into Autumn

MOTHER LAUGHING

Stand at the sink and pull strawberries from a green basket, cut them with a butter knife, sprinkle sugar, mash them in a bowl and sigh. Look out the window at the same empty street. Look at these sundae cups that were stored in a box in the garage. You like them. You never saw them before your mother died. You wish you could ask her about them. These thick glass cups must have belonged to your Grandmother. They're so goddamned beautiful they make you cry. Go to the freezer and get out the ice cream with bits of vanilla bean in it. Roll it with the scoop your mother owned, it's been in the kitchen drawer for at least 40 years. It belongs in your hand. Some things never change. Your fingers look like your mothers. Summer strawberries make ice cream pink. They taste terrific. You eat dessert in front of a television in the house you grew up in. You sit alone in the dark watching *The Munsters*, something funny happens and your mother starts to laugh.

THE MEMORIAL

Everyone knows. No one talks about it
but you, you never stop talking.
You and all your words
add up to exactly nothing.

You said a mouthful
and then you were slapped.
You were beaten by a woman,
keep your big mouth shut.

You don't do grief well—
anger is a part of it.
You don't do anything right
and that makes you angry.

You can't bring yourself to lie, can you?
You stand onstage
at your mother's funeral and ask,
Who were you people, anyway?

It's uncomfortable
this willingness to speak with a choke
on your throat. Uncomfortable feels
like home to you.

Afterwards no one makes eye contact
except a couple of misfits
who shake your hand with their scarred wrists.

The big girl says, *I love you.*
The guy in a dress with mascara running down his cheeks
looks right into you and says, *I know exactly how you feel.*

THERE ARE 27 OBJECTS HIDDEN IN THIS POEM

I can only find seven. A child who is standing
in the background behind the horse distracts me.
The horse is not listed as a hidden object;
neither is the child. I'm not supposed to find them
because they don't count. I can only see part of
the forehead and the hairdo, which is parted
to the side. I think it's a boy but one can't be sure
about gender when someone is young. There are
more than 27 things hidden inside of a child
who isn't listed as hidden. I wonder if the kid is lost.
Children understand lost. I'd imagine this kid would be
easy to relate to if he was willing to relate to the other
children or objects in this poem but I've stopped
looking for objects. I just keep staring at this kid,
which disturbs me, as the author of this piece,
because I know that whatever I think I'm writing
about I'm usually writing about myself.

THE PASSENGER

I like that my father likes me, right now.
I like the way his car smells, exotic and adult.
My dad is playing with his new dentures,
running the tip of his tongue along the top plate
after every sip of beer. He holds a bagged can
with two fingers as he tips it back, just so.
His moves are slow and delicate—
he's been practicing this his entire life—
it's like the way he smokes. He's a professional,
he studies smokers, because it matters.

NIGHT IN TRANSIT

You showed me family photos and said, *this too*.
I remember the way your hands looked
when you showed me a picture of your mother
so I could see how perfect she was
in that wedding dress.

My mother wasn't perfect.
Our relationship was cordial, not close.
I left home when I was in high school
and started sleeping in my car.
I didn't expect to feel anything
when my mother died
but I cried like a child
startled by grief.

After I told you this
you told me about your father,
about what he did to you,
and why you never talk to him.

I fell asleep just after midnight.
Part of me slept on your futon in New York City.
Part of me slept in a bed with my wife.
Part of me slept with the tomatoes in our yard.
Part of me slept on the bottom bunk;
my parents were right down the hall.

What was left of me woke up at 4 a.m.
in the back of a 1962 Plymouth station wagon.
I was exhausted when I rose from sleep.
I was sweaty, it was humid
and I needed a shower.

I stepped into your moonlit bathroom
and saw the ghost tub, a porcelain nude reclining
with its curved skin and cold claw feet.
I stripped off my clothes and stepped into your tub.

Every time I took a breath that day
I thought about my mother.
I pressed my face into the water
that tumbled from your showerhead.
I stood there for a long time—
feeling how it felt—
and I wondered what I would look like
when I stepped out of this kiln.

THE ONE ABOUT THE BATHTUB

I've heard that if one travels deep into the ocean they will experience weightlessness. No one has to tell me about the gravity in a bathtub. They don't warn you enough about unprotected bathing. I know you can't get pregnant from a person's hand but once it gets inside you it's there. A bathtub is not like an ocean; it's a place where a human body can sink like an anchor.

FOR THE BIRDS

Some say if you touch a baby bird you kill it. Some say it depends on whether you use a hand or a wing. Some say why did you touch the chick and where? Some say you have to be punished to learn. It takes a hard hand to raise a creature from the nest. Some birds get thrown into the pool just to see if they will sink or swim. Some say it takes a witch. Some say it takes a devil to make a bird fear God. Some grow up to say *I don't care what you say.* Some birds scream like a boiling kettle until you turn off the heat.

COYOTE MOON

This week we arrived at a work-comp settlement,
or settled for what we are going to get;
we're getting one third of one year's income.
I juiced greens, did the dishes, gimped around the house
and accepted what I cannot change. I accept what this is.
I'd grown miserable in the position I was in.
I'm below the poverty line now, but I'm happier.

A coyote walked down the middle of our street
in the middle of the day, only yesterday.
My dog started to bark-whine
and I went to see what was wrong.
There was nothing but a window screen
separating my dog and a coyote.
The coyote looked well fed.
It stood in our front yard and sniffed the air.
I picked my dog up; we looked out the window together.
The coyote appeared to be smiling
as it turned and walked away.

This afternoon, after I signed the settlement papers,
Lori retired to the bedroom to huddle under blankets.
She stayed under most of the day,
only getting up once or twice
to tell me that she did not want to live,
because life isn't fair.
She pointed out that the two of us
would be driving used cars into our graves.

Lori got out of bed last night,
right after the sun went down.
We stood in the front yard and looked at the full moon.
It was huge.
It feels like fall, I said.
Yeah, she said, *but it looks a little off around the edges.*
I accepted that and went back into the house.

Last night, right after I fell asleep, I was two inches tall.
I watched myself walk on a six-by-twenty-foot conveyor.
This conveyor belt led to the paper grinder.
The grinder was rumbling but there was no paper on the belt.
I was alone in the recycling plant.
I was certain I had forgotten something.
My equipment was up and running.
I knew the crew should be around here somewhere.
Something was wrong. Was it something I did,
or something I didn't do?
I knew I was supposed to be somewhere
doing something. I kept on walking the conveyor.
Was I supposed to be at the courthouse?
Then, suddenly, I wasn't on a conveyor at all,
I was in my maintenance cage
wiping grease from my hand tools.
My boss started yelling at me like I was his dog,
Stay! You stay!
I looked at my toolbox as I answered him,
I can't stay; I have to go to court.
Then he asked, in anger, *When are you going to wake up?*

Tonight, I'm sitting at the back porch, listening to the rain.
Lori is angry at me because I don't fight back.
I'm not angry.
I moved on and the fight moved behind me;
it's cold out here and I can't see the moon.

I'M SURE I WANT TO DO THIS

1.
She never cuts her hair. I mean, she never had it cut short. She could have, with a face like that. She could have done whatever she wanted with hair like that, and her sweet swayback.

Is there another poem in the way she walks, or how she is with children, or grandchildren? Should I write a poem about us in bed, lying on our backs as she swims through the change in a pool of sweat, with a fan blowing on her pretty face, her body awash in moonlight?

Should I write about myself, wide awake, floating in a pool of worries, my shoulders no longer able to swim, my ankle swollen, my back arthritic? My chest, once stitched, has never been the same.

I look at the ceiling. I listen to you. You have no idea how hard it is to fall asleep and not hear you breathing. Should I write about how I watch you sleep, because of your face and how good it makes me feel?

I love your hot flashes, you are not inclined to wear much and less is more. All I wanted was to mate for life. I keep checking to make sure you are still here. Look what happened to us. Look at the life that came to me through you.

2.
A gray-haired woman pats my shoulder saying, *Today is Sunday, did you remember to take your medicine?* I am finally forgetting what day it is. I lean my head against her right breast. We had some good sex; maybe that's the key. My pulse is blushing faster now. *What about your heart?* she says, as she pinches and pulls on my earlobe. *Are you sure you want to do this? What about your back,* she asks, *and what about your leg?*

KEN

A man parks his walker and sits down at a fast food diner table. He says a prayer, unwraps his burger and forgets to eat. He stares at the framed photo he's placed on the table. He stares for a while, burger in hand. He listens to this woman like he used to listen to the radio. She can make him laugh; she can make him cry. He doesn't feel like eating today but she tells him he has to. She never liked this place but now she goes where he goes, waits patiently in a photograph and smiles at him while he eats.

NOTE TO SELF

Be thankful for the dishes waiting to be washed.
Be thankful you are not alone in your car
unwrapping a meal under parking lot lights.
Be thankful you can feel the pain
that stabs your back when you rise
to meet the day. Be thankful
when you put on your own pants, one leg at a time
because nothing lasts forever. The day is coming
when you will no longer be able
to tie your own shoes. You will know something
is wrong but you will not be able recognize your own
hunger. Be thankful she is there to feed you,
forgive you and remember your name
after you have forgotten hers.

FOR THE ATTENDANT WHO CHANGES ME

It used to frighten me when I tried to remember
what was there before the bird flew away. I stare
into the blankness where words were. **Wall**
I remember, they call that thing a **Wall**.

Stand, she says, *can you stand by yourself?* I don't
always hold on to the thing. I can't let that trouble
me. It comes to me, this thing where my things are.
My things are in there. She is going to dress me. Now
I remember, this thing is called a **Dress**. I nod my head
and speak; it comes out weaker than a whisper.
I don't know why I say *yes*, I meant to say *dress*.

It takes a long time for a word to illuminate
and disappear before it gets out of my mouth.
Some things can't remain in words; sometimes
I cup the word and swallow it like a pill.
This time I said it. I said *yes*. I don't know why I said *yes*
when I meant to say **Dresser**.

My voice is going away. I have thoughts sometimes
and I'm staring at the wall when she rips the tabs on my **Diaper**.
I'm wearing a **Diaper** when I realize and the **Wall** begins to move
sideways.

> *I'm not holding on to anything as I walk on the beach*
> *with my hair on fire. The wind is blowing on the flames*
> *but they don't go out. I dive into the water but I stay in the air.*
> *I'm surprised how easy it is to fly over the rose bushes.*

My cheekbone barks like a **Dog**.
I feel my face crack like a **Spider Web**.
My cheek begins to **Whistle** like a **Bullet Hole** in a **Pane of Glass**.
This is just like the movie I saw where the guy got hit on the **Noggin**
and the words came back. I'm better now. I remember everything.

The girl is **Frantic**.
I'm staring at the **Ceiling**.
I'm lying on the **Threshold** to the **Bathroom**. I start talking to myself.
I say, *I'm so hungry I could eat a **horse***. Where did that come from? Why did I say that?
I'm a **Vegetarian**. I don't eat **Meat**.

THE GHOST

My mother has died but she hasn't left
my dorm room, a long cell-like chamber
where the box fan never stops humming,
the noise never leaves my window
and I don't think my mother will go
until I acknowledge her, she badgers me
to accept her forgiveness or to forgive her,
I'm not sure I know the difference. I can't
see her and even though she can't speak
to me, she keeps trying. I was trained
to apologize at a young age and will
apologize to anyone for almost anything
that happens and even for what doesn't.
I'm always sorry but I can't say I'm sorry
to an apparition, not unless I really mean it,
because spirits see right through me. I lie
on the bed for hours with her ghost hovering
above me, remembering. I've always been
of two minds about remembering. I can't
remember everything she said but I know
before she started slapping she often said,
I'll give you something to cry about.
The odd thing is I never cried, and now,
when I start to cry I feel embarrassed.
I was taught not to feel sorry for myself.
I can't remember what was said when she was
slapping my face but I remember some of what
she said when she pounded my back. She used
to tell me I would never amount to anything
and I've always believed her. I remember her
saying that if I thought things were tough
around here I should wait until I grow up
and get out there. She often finished up by
saying for my 18th birthday she was buying me
two suitcases and a kick in the ass. Then she'd
literally kick me, for emphasis, like a punch line.
People don't know about this. I'm sorry.
I don't know why I never told anybody.

THE DEAD

I spoke to the night sky   words were never enough   I spoke them anyway
I was not dead   I hoped to find her   I was unaware   at first   but she
began to follow me   she came back   between breaking waves   when
I listened to music   I could not help but cry   on trains in buses in
classrooms full of students   I was not alone   I began to recognize
others   shivering like Autumn leaves   carrying dead parents   in
the corners of their eyes

MOTHER

I'm alone
I don't want sleep

how can I eat
I breathe

my heart is beating
like a candle flame

the sun comes up
on the backs of birds

oh my bones
my hollow bones

birth is loss
death is birth

you are the mist
that buries these hills

BALLOON MOON

Old moon,
the distance between us is greater than us.

What I once felt,
I no longer feel. You seem far away,

like something I never loved,
like someone I never knew.

My hand lets go of the string.
You are lighter than air.

POODLE NURSE

My head is dizzy after rolling out of bed, relying on the elbow and the hip until I get one foot on the floor. Sometimes I have to sit on the edge for a second or two and collect my bearings before trying to stand up, get dressed and go for a walk. Sometimes my heart forgets how to do the dance and does a couple of quick missteps. My heart knows that the new pig valve is not one of my body parts.

Pearl and I have been walking for more than an hour. My breath is shorter this week because my chest is sore. Sometimes it blooms into a bruise only I can see. My running shoes were spotless from the gym but now they are muddy and rain spotted from chasing park ducks back into the creek. Ducks will go where my dog says they should go. When we run towards them they regroup and waddle, quacking amongst themselves. Pearl has learned that if she barks real loud and stands up on her hind legs she can make ducks fly. That's a lot of power.

My shirt is damp with perspiration, so is my hair. I'd rather walk but Pearl wants to run straight up the hill to the parking lot. Who I am to resist joy? When Pearl runs she turns into a rabbit, not just running but launching her seven pounds with back legs bounding.

Pearl bounces across to the passenger side as soon as I open the car door. I'm breathing so hard that Pearl becomes concerned. Pearl has been my nurse for the last three months. She places a paw on my arm and waits for me to collect myself. Then she licks the backside of my hand, several times. That's the medicine for this situation and it works.

THIS IS NOT A PIPE MOON

Clouds like train smoke puffing
one after the other are sucked back
into the night. The moon curls
across the sky in the bright tonight,
the moon is beaming.

Clouds lit up, floating around, have no idea
it's the middle of the night. They make my lawn
chair tilt. I sit and watch the slow parade.

Clouds of glory, impregnated with rain,
swim like fish. White dog on a dark lawn
watches clouds float in a wading pool.

Some clouds spin cotton,
some drift smoke,
some sprinkle salt…

My face was lit up like a cloud.
My cheeks were pulled like taffy. I fell apart.
My jaw dropped from my skull. My head stretched wider
than a crocodile's smile. My hair wandered off in wisps.

I am a songless bird, a blank face, an empty beak…

The moon stares directly into the sun.
The moon is blind like love is blind.
Maybe this is not the moon
burning in the bowl of Magritte's pipe.

MOTHER LOSING HER MIND

When my mother started losing her mind
she couldn't remember the people

in her photo albums which was a blessing
because most of them had died.

She wasn't sure how she hurt herself
but seeing blood was frightening.

She couldn't stop looking for her car keys
even though she couldn't drive.

When we moved her to assisted living,
one by one her children's faces departed.

She allowed her body to surrender to gravity
and slowly sank into the deep end.

She began to walk in short steps, like a Geisha,
then she forgot how to walk.

One day my mother couldn't remember
how to eat,

she stared at the food on her plate
and wondered what the fork was for.

Today, my mother is content,
she sits in her wheelchair and stares,

she surrounds herself in silence.
All she is, is now.

MY WIFE TALKS TO STRANGERS

My wife stopped the cart in the produce section
and began talking to a woman she's never seen before
about my issues with anger. This stranger happened
to know a therapist who is good at helping people
like me get in touch with their inner child.
She agrees with my wife; I do need help. This woman
I don't know jots down a phone number I can call,
when I'm ready.

Moments later, my wife strikes up a conversation
with a homeless man in the parking lot.
As she gives him a dollar she points to me
and tells him I had heart surgery recently,
just like Rob Lowe in that television show.
I'm stand there listening to her tell a total stranger
about our viewing habits, about how we don't watch
the same shows and how I should get a day planner
because I am getting old and I forget things.

While we are driving home, she tells me stories
about people I don't know. When she recalls a scene
she assumes I've seen it too, even if I wasn't there.
Her life is centered on people. The truth is, I don't care
about other people's lives. My mind is occupied with things
I read in books. I'd rather talk to my dog than talk to a person
and I'm a pretty good listener when my dog talks to me.

When we got home I told my dog that it makes me angry
when my wife tells strangers that I need help.
My dog suggested we have a snack and then go for a walk.
That was good advice and it made me feel better.

APRIL

1.
It's been a while since I spent my time
staring at the activity outside my hospital window—
a seventh-story window—
facing a parking lot below;
a window that would not open
because nurses never know
when a patient will discover how they really feel.

2.
I took long walks down short hallways
lined with beige doors, walls interrupted
by neutral art, fruit in baskets,
earth-tone landscapes, calm colors captured
in whitewash frames.
There was always at least one cop
sitting on a folding chair
at the end of my hallway
outside of a patient's door.
I never found out which side of the law
that patient was on,
or what sort of secret
those cops were guarding.

3.
My constant companion
was an antibiotic drip bag
hung from a metal pole.
We took walks together.

The nurses kept moving my IV needle.
One by one, my veins collapsed;
I was bruised on both sides of my wrists;
one morning a nurse missed the vein
in my right hand; she pierced a nerve;
the electrical current pricked a path
up my arm and out the back-end of my elbow.
I watched my hand puff up.

When I could no longer make a fist,
I called for the nurse. She was kind to me,
she removed the needle.
She told me she would give my veins a rest
for an hour or two.
No longer tied to an IV pole,
I put on pajama pants and a tee shirt,
grabbed a five-dollar bill from the nightstand
and headed for the elevator.
I rode it to the first floor
where I bought a cup of coffee at the gift shop.

I stepped outside and looked up.
I felt air touch my skin.
Have you gone without food for days?
Do you remember how it felt to eat?
Standing outside was that kind of good to me.

A woman rolled up in a wheelchair,
she waited at the curb with a newborn in her arms.
She made cooing noises and adjusted a baby blanket
while an attendant stood behind her.

A young man entered the glass doors of the building;
a Mylar balloon festooned with flowers followed him.
I tossed the remainder of my coffee into a trash can.
I also went inside. When I returned to the seventh floor
things had changed. The nurses began watching me.
The nurse who had been kind to me
wheeled an IV stand into my room.
She silently pushed an IV needle into my neck vein,
then she taped a plastic tube to my shoulder,
close to the collarbone.

4.
The plant was down so we weren't taking breaks;
the bosses were working us as fast as they could;
we were dripping sweat;
we were smeared with machine oil;
four of us disassembled the shredder;
we removed steel plates and stacked them on a pallet,
raised on forks to knee height.

Each plate was one inch thick; the edges were sharp;
they were heavy; we could barely fit four to a layer.
We dropped one plate at each corner of the pallet
until the four stacks were 20 plates high.
I dropped the 21st plate on the corner closest to me
and turned my back on the pallet. I heard the pallet break
as twenty greased plates slid through the air
and collided with the back of my leg.
The top plate made a cut into my right calf.
It made a triangular flap of my meat.
I was in shock. I could see my tendons.
The company doctor gave me twenty-five stitches,
one bottle of pain pills and a note
which sent me back to work.

Things went from bad to worse. I left that job.
Now I talk to doctors, therapists and attorneys.
They ask about the pain, on a scale of one to ten.
They ask about my ability to perform my job.
They never ask me how it felt to stop dancing.

5.
The woman in the next room never left her bed.
Her door was always open; she had a lot of visitors;
on the sixth day they came and went all day,
a parade of weepers. On Sunday morning,
the bed was made and the woman was not in it.
The parking lot was empty.
I sat in my room with nothing to distract me.
I can only read books for so long.
I need to learn to sit and feel.

6.
Now I have time to spend with my dog.
She is always sitting on my lap, protecting my body.
I don't have to tell her; she knows where I hurt.
Tonight, she is sniffing the air,
keeping a watch over every inch of lawn.
I stare at the full moon. I am not feeling pain.
I have a good dog. I tell her that several times a day.

ALZHEIMER'S YARD

Just above
the locked fence
my mother's mind
is blazing blue.
Clouds appear
to have faces
and she wants
to give them names.
My mother points
a finger at the sky
and almost speaks
but words don't come,
or words can't get out,
it really doesn't matter.
That cloud isn't the same
cloud. It changed. Now
it looks like someone else.

VISITING MOTHER

Her hands close and pull at the air just inches from my neck. She reaches for long strands but I've cut my hair short. She knows me from somewhere but that was a lifetime ago. She takes my hand in both of hers. Her hands are wrinkled, her skin is thin and her veins are blue. She searches my eyes, trying to place me. I ask her if she likes living in this place. She says she is worried about lunch.

We pass a piano on the way to the cafeteria where she stops to gaze at the keys. I know by her face that her hands remember. She tells me about dances that she used to go to with her husband. His name is Ken. Every man she dances with is Ken. Ken is every man she ever married and every man she dreams about. She points to a resident shuffling down the hall. *There he goes*, my mother says, *that's my Ken*, and she follows him.

JUNKYARD MOON

I don't know what to say about this new moon.
I've seen it before. It looks like a television rerun.
I planted seeds and waited for rain to come but it didn't.
I don't know if the weatherman lied or if he didn't know
the truth. One by one my used cars died and were buried
in junkyards stripped of stereos and speakers. Sing to me,
be straight with me, tell me who you really are
and I will cling to every word like moss, like a baby,
like a leech.

My shadow has passed through thousands of thresholds.
My shadow followed me down this dark alley.
My silhouette is stooped, hands raised above its head.
I am not ready for this. All of a sudden, I'm stopped.
My wheels won't turn. No check in the mail.
No reason for alarm. Nobody cares what I do.
I can sleep now. I can sleep for as long as I like.

THE BLIGHT

It's hard to believe anything ever grew here.

I turn my spade to the ground, loosen dirt, remove weeds and add warm bags of soil but as soon as tomatoes or flowers appear their leaves turn hard and yellow.

I showed some of these leaves to the old guy at the nursery and he said I had the blight.

I asked what to do. He said *there's nothing can be done because it's the blight. It's like the flu,* he said. *It flies through the air and hides in your drinking water. It lives on your hands and you pass it to whatever you touch.*

STRAWBERRIES IN SPRING

strawberries in spring
grow small, hard,
green and timid

seeds small as ground pepper
bloom like blemishes
on pale knuckle bodies

the pulse of larva waiting
for the blood of summer to blush
in what must be their faces

soon you will find them
sprouting green hats
hanging on stems

that stand up erect
and point to the sky
like feathers

I AM READY TO LISTEN WHEN YOU ARE READY TO TALK

The cookies in the jar are waiting for us. Here we go dropping crumbs, walking deep into the woods. We are ready for anything. The yard birds greet the morning and the morning is ready for us. Here we go but we go by fast. We are ready to decant a decent wine. We are not ready for what is ready for us. Here we go but here we stay. I am ready to listen to you read your poem. The front door is open and ready for me. Here we go again, let's do this together. I am ready to dance if the dance is with you. The dog in my chair is waiting for me. Here we go, I say to my daughter as she takes her first step. I am ready for the turtle doves to return and nest again. I reach for your hand and you are ready for me. Here we go, etching names in the bark of the mulberry tree. I am ready to not say anything. Just put on that dress and get ready for me. Here we go, I say to the poodle as we stick the shift. I am ready to pull away from the curb. I apologized and you were kind to me. Here we go on sidewalks and here we go on trains. I am ready for some merrymaking. The books on my shelf can wait for me. Here we go with legs that work and bodies that swagger sway. I am ready to let you drive. Tomato plants are buzzed by bees, the yellow flowers wink at me. Here we go, holding on for dear life as our planet spins in space. I am ready for the end of wars. I knock on death's door and death is waiting for us. Here we go, we can't go back. I am ready to call you beautiful. I did not plan this but this was always ready for us. Here we go, singing hallelujahs with polished plates of sunlight haloed high above our heads.

OUTSIDE

A red-tailed hawk with wings spread
was gliding overhead,
as we walked the narrow trail
into the shadow canyon, and she said,
That's what we need, clear oxygen.

And that's what we'd been missing.
Walking helps me remember.
I remember when we could see the stars
all night long if we wanted,
or papoose the twins and walk
up Cow Mountain, if we wanted.

I remember driving slow down Talmage Road
that autumn, when grape leaves turned
the color of wine, nobody but us drove that road
and we could drive as slow as we wanted.

I remember red clay sticking to my boots
as we walked the trails on the Greenwood Ridge,
the way those mountains talked to us,
and emptied us,
and filled us.

There is nothing better than cool green air
in my nose, in my ears,
deep in the hollow, just past the ferns.

BABY PICTURE

You are bundled in a blanket, wrapped tight because of colic. Your toothless mouth is open. Your hand is out of the blanket but your elbow is trapped. Your fingers are small. Your fingernails shine like Scotch tape. Your curling hand is almost a fist. Your entire being is focused on the distance between hand and mouth. You are thinking all the time, about air, light, sound, smell, all sorts of things in the world around you. I suspect you are only self-aware when you hunger for your mother's breast, for the suck of your own hand, or for someone like me to hold you. You are lying on our couch, inches away from your brother. You are the small twin, five minutes behind the other. You have been dealt a hand. Nobody can see what cards you are holding. Nobody knows what happens next. Everything is new to both of us.

WHAT I WANT

I want to stop you here
at the intersection of was and when,
in the moment of neither here nor there,
where you are always standing with your head lifted
to the light, waiting for the signal to change.

I will hold that moment inside of me
like a Gustav Klimt painting.
I want to lie you down on the grass,
close you in my eyes and etch flecks gold
into every one of your shadows.

That's what I want. I want you,
with plenty of flowers.

FLOWER CHILD

I was a handle in search of a plow
I was a hunger in need of a horse
I was a huntsman, a bringer of seeds

She was the bluebird on God's green shoulder
She was born a broken promise
She brought stories to the fire

Once upon a time she spent her time
liberating flowers from rich folk's gardens
Flowers were the money she was planning to spend

She broke loose in a puff of smoke
She went flying on a flick of ash
She went winding down a mountain road
She rode the skids on a hair-pin curve

She was a fast driver
She was a good girl with really great hair
She was a glimpse of heaven in a see-through top

When we met, we just were
it just was, and it was good
and all of a sudden we were always there

Once her porch-light eyes came on for me
Once she started calling me home
Once I fell in love with her beautiful face
Once upon a time we both looked good
Once it happened we didn't even blink

We could make a black couch blush
We hit it so hard we popped out the shower doors
We did it in the garden and we did it on the mountain
We did it by the lake and we did it in the water
We made the blue sky blue
We did it and we did it and we had twin sons

Pink blossoms bloomed in the almond tree
We did it again and had a baby girl
Flower petals fell and landed in our yard
Flower petals landed on the footpath to her door
Flower petals fell and planted perfume at her feet

WE CALLED IT THE BRIGHT SPOT

Because we were stupid.
The irony of our situation was lost on us
and we were lost on each other.
It's not like I was hiding. No one was looking for me
I didn't own a wristwatch, didn't have an address
to give to a potential employer.

I grew tired of hitchhiking and settled down.
If anyone wanted to find me, they could find me
in the basement of the Unitarian Church
where I made coffee and sold fruit from a wooden bowl.
I took tips from anyone who was willing.

I took girls to my room and read them notebook poems.
I was skin and bone. My pants were getting looser.
I was taking whites, the kind with the cross
stamped in the center. The kind that cost a dime
rolled ten to a line. The kind that kept my tongue
exploring my inner cheek. I chewed enamel off my teeth.

I was shrunk like a mouse in a hamster wheel.
I wrote with the strength of a thousand men.
That was me. I tore down the factory.
I swam upstream like a fire escape.
I didn't give a fuck what you thought.

I was an uncontrollable man. Nobody told me what to do
I was a stain, a used mattress dropped on an un-swept floor.
I never turned my back on you. Whenever I locked my door
the silence that filled my ears was you.

INFIDEL

You are an empty vessel
docked on a body of water

a passenger in a parking lot
of ships leashed to moorings

the waves are small as babies
that rock you side to side

your flowers bruised
your body drained of tears

your hands get busy
covering your eyes
covering your mouth
covering your ears

things have gone bananas
but this is your monkey
your trouble your chance
to adapt and survive

you sleep like a bat
in the back of a cave
you fly in the blackness
navigating your dreams

surrounded by echoes
that bounce off fixed objects
a series of shadows
will stand in your way

AMERICAN MOON

You are calm, cool,
the ice that drifts in my drink.

I reach for you,
squeeze you in my fist.

You are bigger than my life
and smaller than my thumb.

The moon should be thankful
it doesn't live here.

The moon is far away.
I decide to go there.

I climb out of my spaceship
and do a zero-gravity dance.

I poke around the moon in a tin foil suit
with my stiff little flag.

I have no business on the moon.
I stare at the earth, the earth stares back.

This is how it is to be alone.
I have no language to speak of here.

The moon is bathed in silence,
silence bathed in light.

DEATH IN THE VILLAGE
after Elana Bell

When you drown the child in the wading pool he begs you NO with his black, black eyes. The plastic pool is cheerful blue. If the sky was a coin that landed on your lawn it would come up this shade of blue. The face on the coin is like the face in the mirror in a service station bathroom. Stare at it long enough and the mirror stops breathing. Light leaks and outlines the edges of a body. Everyone has an aura, even you.

THE FIRST TIME

was in a bar in the back of a car during the war my father took me to a house he was drunk I was stoned it was early she was late it was the baby sitter it was my uncle crying I don't know how it happened I was just a kid and didn't know what was what or what went where or why or how these things were supposed to fit together.

THE PASSENGER

Increase your bet by two's, every second time you win, like this: 2, 4, 8, 16, 32, 64... you got the idea? Get beyond a stack of 128 and you will have a night to remember, my father says, as he tousles my hair.

I like it when he tousles my hair.

When you bet the big stack, you make the dealer nervous. Make her look over her shoulder for the pit boss. Enjoy the game. Own the dealer and you own the moment. Never forget this son, the dealer is your enemy. She is working for the house.

The Grand Prix has been speeding up as he tells his story. He sits at a card table, his face lit by dashboard lights. The blinker blinks as he turns to park on Mom's front lawn. He parks the Grand Prix a few inches from the front porch.

BLOOD MOON

Today was sheltered in a marine layer; we waded through a sea without shadows.

Today I made a donation for the funeral of a friend killed by a drunk driver.

I watched a mouse escape from my dog.

I watched pink feet, a black fur blur scrambling across concrete with its tiny life.

Tonight. I saw the moon poke its face out from behind the clouds as a black mist rose up like a cape to cover the chin, the lips, the teeth…

Lori asked me, *Does the moon always show us the same face? Does it sometimes show us its other faces?*

I don't know, I said and we marveled at how clouds had misshapen the moon's skull until it looked dented and pockmarked like it had been kicked and kicked repeatedly.

Feral kittens under my house began to yowl.

My dog ran zig-zags and barked and barked and barked.

A mouse squeezed her body into a hole in a brick wall—a tight passage—small as a pencil spine. Then it was gone.

No light twinkled. The moon turned dark as a dime dropped down a slot.

THE DARK

1.
My family, in a tight circle
gazed across the bonfire ring.

My mother's hair was full of sparks,
her eyes were raw as onions.

The sand began to moan and move beneath my feet
but I rode it like a wave.

The sky started falling
out of both sides of her mouth.

The hills behind my heart
were blooming heat,

My impaled marshmallow
began to turn,

from soft skin to scab,
from stiff skin to pus,

all of our coat hangers
were glowing.

2.
Twenty years have passed.
I am half asleep

on my bed, a gun
sticking out of my mouth.

She asks, *Are you dreaming?*
She asks, *How have you been sleeping?*

Off and on, I think,
all things come and go.

A fire burns in my chest.
I've been feeding it.

It takes something away
every time I breathe.

I slide down deeper underneath the blanket.
Where are you going?

My mother's disembodied voice asks,
Where have you been?

Once again,
the wind approaches like a whore,

no one summons it
but the fire loves it.

Half-awake now, my mind drifts
with a car, into opposing traffic.

The bed jerks and I startle her.
This is real.

I keep hurting myself.
Now the fire has spread

to the hills behind the highway,
the waves are breaking,

the wind is singing
and it just won't stop.

HIS MARBLES

A man collects his marbles in the hope that it will make him sane. Soon enough, his pants pockets are full of marbles. Marbles leave dents in his thighs, his pants pockets swell under increasing pressure, his fly will not stay zipped but he can't stop adding marbles to his pockets. There is always room for one more marble.

One day the marble man strikes up a conversation with a cat lady. She is sitting in the alleyway on an abandoned couch. Cats have used the couch as a scratching post. Shredded fabric floats in the air around her like prayer flags. She calls her cats by name and they come to her. Jamal and Teresa sit on her lap. Teresa has an eye infection and Jamal has a toothache. The cat lady's clothes are covered in cat hair; she is soft and warm like a comfortable sweater. This woman is the Mother Teresa of cats, not the Virgin Mary of cats. The marble man finds the cat lady surprisingly attractive. She makes him awkward and tongue-tied. He's unable to speak well, or think straight, and this makes him appear to be a good listener. The cat lady enjoys his attentions, she thinks he's cute and she asks him to sit down and stay a while. He wants to sit beside her in the worst way but he can't because his pants are tight and it hurts to sit down when your pockets are stuffed with marbles.

That night the marble collector falls asleep in a single bed and dreams he has been set free. He starts reaching into his pockets and tosses fistfuls of marbles into the air. Marbles flock in the air like small tropical birds. Marbles drop and ping on the floor until they form a colorful moat around him. Soon the marbles stop bouncing and the room is painfully silent. The marble collector stands in the center of the circle of marbles and zips up his fly. His pants are loose and carefree. He is finally happy. He thinks about the cat lady and knows he must join her but he is trapped inside the circle of marbles. Every step he is followed by a pratfall because man is not made to walk on marbles. He slips and flips and trips and falls and falls again. God is always watching us and God loves a good pratfall. God laughs until it hurts because the guy with all the marbles is funny.

YOU ARE MY SUNSHINE
after Paul Botello

A man sits alone in his head and remembers a woman who comes to him when a black cat arches its back against the man's pant leg. The woman in a blue dress sits on his lap and brings her mouth close his mouth. He can feel her breathing. This wakes the boy at his side, the boy who always wanted the girl to kiss him. Her skeleton has left her body but she is still soft and warm. The sun and moon do a dance in the window. Green vines embrace her bones.

RUNNING AWAY FROM HOME

Over my shoulder, perched in a tree,
my mother was watching me.

I looked back and said,
Why don't you leave me alone?

I knew she could hear me.
She always acted like I wasn't there.

Go Away, I said, again and again.
I began to cry with a voice that wasn't mine.

That frantic woman kept throwing herself
against the bars of my cage.

I kept walking.
I looked down, not up, when I talked to my mother.

The air was full of feathers.
I was full of me.

I could not let her in.

A WOMAN CAN'T HOLD ALL THE STORM IN HER HEAD
after Carmen Gimenez Smith

It's in her head. It's all in her head and she surrenders to it. She sees a flash of light before she hears the thunder. Her windows begin to tremble. The rain is outside this house but if she stays indoors it can't get to her. The storm is hitting her roof. She can hear the droplets bouncing like children on furniture and it frightens her.

You have no idea what it's like to be a mother but you can understand how easy it is to break things—be it bones, or blue plates—take care to preserve what you have because it's not a set anymore when you start losing pieces.

THE PASSENGER

He kills the engine. We sit together in silence in front of my mother's house and my father says it again, just before he leaves. *Own the dealer, that's what this is about. When you finally lose a hand, go back to your initial bet. Push in two dollars, after you've taken hundreds of dollars from the house, look her straight in the eye and make sure she knows who won. Never tip the dealer or apologize. Don't be weak, son, not when you're winning.*

EVERYBODY KNOWS A WOLF CAN'T SMILE

A wolf walks at her side, growing with the shadows, stretching his big bad self across the woods, loping smoothly with a six-tree stride. The fur on his back is wild and electric, not soft and pretty like the hair that slips in haphazard curls from between Red's hood and cape. The wolf has forgotten about the basket of goodies and is fixated on the scent of little girl blood. His paws move silently. His ears stand erect. He focuses on footsteps, twigs snapping and the commingling of breath that joins the girl to the animal. Look at the moon resting on Red's riding hood as if she were the source of light and look at the wolf, housed in darkness, hidden by trees, his eyes lit bright and yellow like a blackbird that waits and watches and smiles.

GRACE

We folded our hands like white bread
We gave thanks for family dinner
Our Father, full of space
Hail Mary, full of grace
The Lord had the blues

The dinner table had chrome fenders and legs
We leaned into our food with hunched backs
We squeaked and scooted on vinyl chairs

We sang *bless us oh Lord, bless these, thy gifts*
It was crowded at the table
Christ crucified hung on the wall
Jesus with his two-fingered wave
Jesus with his open-heart chest

The food was bad
First it was bloody
Then it was dry
I was a good boy
I ate my vegetables

I sang *This Little Heart of Mine*
I sang *In-A-Gadda-Da-Vida*
Dinner was elbow to elbow
Dinner was every one for himself
I was a kid, I never saw anybody else
All I knew about others was what they did to me

Blessed art now amongst sinners
With mutiny on the bounty
Through Christ our Lord
Amen

CHURCH

Jesus hangs above the altar,
pinned like a butterfly,
barbed wire thorns circle his head.
His arms are outstretched
like he's going to hug everybody.
Stained glass saints go about their business.
Parishioners file in and wait for Jesus,
hymnals are shelved on the backs of pews,
thin veils cover women's heads,
I stare at the backs of their naked necks.

A priest comes out and does the thing—
we stand we sit,
we kneel we pray.

Jesus hides in a tray of money.
Jesus does the backstroke in a glass of wine,
he abides in a loaf of bread,
he snaps his bloody fingers,
spreads his bloody wings
and floats on his cross forever
on a stage in a room with no wind.

THE ALTAR BOY

Sky drops a hand on my forehead

I dream out the window

All these years like flown birds

Parishioners pass

They pass like fence posts

Priest in a robe, in a hat, in black

I hold a gold tray

I stand three paces behind

The priest presses the moon on tongue after tongue

Saints burn like candles in the windows

THE SANDBOX

I traveled over roads I carved with my fingers. I pressed Tonka treads across hills and valleys. I wore out that truck and it felt good in my hands. I don't know if I spoke to my toy or if it spoke to me, but we talked, every day. When my truck died I dug a grave in the sand and buried it. I picked some weeds to place on its chest, made a cross out of popsicle sticks and said a prayer: *Here is your god. Here is your grave. There you go, now you are dead.* My hands were always dirty. I rubbed my fingers against my eyelids and watched specks sparkle inside the darkness of me.

Daniel McGinn is a native of Whittier, California. He's led writing workshops at Half Off Books, The Orange County Rescue Mission, charter schools and poetry venues. Daniel received his MFA in writing from Vermont College of Fine Arts. Write Bloody published his first full-length collection of poetry, *1000 Black Umbrellas*. Five of his chapbooks were included in the Laguna Poets Series. Daniel has been a regular contributor to *Next Magazine* and the *O.C. Weekly*, he also curated a reading series at Bean's Coffee House in Whittier, California, and was a member a member of the 1996 Los Angeles national Slam team. Daniel has been married to the poet and painter, Lori McGinn, for 41 years.

ACKNOWLEDGEMENTS

Versions of these poems have appeared in:

Sadie Girl anthologies (*Incandescent Mind Vol.1, 2 and 3,*
 Then & Now, and *Like a Girl*)
Silver Birch Press website and anthologies (*Summer, Ides,*
 and the chapbook, *13 Moons*)
For the Love of Words anthologies (*Short Poems Ain't Got Nobody to*
 Love, Attack of The Poems, and *A Poet is a Poet No Matter How Tall*)
Lucid Moose (*Gutters and Alleyways: Perspectives on Poverty and Struggle*)
Cadence Collective website and Cadence Collective anthologies Vol. 1 and 2
Black Napkin
Amethyst Arsenic
Lummox
Inevitable Press (*Wall*)
Write Bloody (*We Will Be Shelter*)
Bank Heavy (*Donut Touch Me*)
Drunk In A Midnight Choir Webzine
Spectrum 9
IndeFeed podcast

The author would like to thank:

Ralph Angel, Mary Rueful, Matthew Dickman, Mark Cox, Betsy Sholl, and Richard McMann for mentoring me at Vermont College of Fine Arts.

Bonnie Saunders and Leslie Mary Ann Neil for proofreading and editing suggestions on poems included in this manuscript.

G. Murray Thomas for *Next Magazine*, his Murrayness, and all the good things he's done for Southern California poetry. Pat, Marcia, and Devin for Laguna Poets, Lob, Victor, Mindy, Beth, and Elmo for the Java Garden, Michael Paul for being my co-host at Beans, Mifanwy for Tebot Bach, John for the Brew Pub, Lee and Jaimes for the Gypsy Dens, Ben and Steve for the Ugly Mug, Joanne and Ed for Pondwater, Danielle for The Poetry Lab, Brendan for hosting workshops all over town, Nicelle for publishing my work in gumball machines, on water bottles, trading cards, hats and umbrellas, Derrick for publishing my first full-length collection, Rachel for loving Lori and I and becoming part of our family.

PATRONS

Moon Tide Press would like to thank the following people for their support in helping publish the finest poetry from the Southern California region. To sign up as a patron, visit www.moontidepress.com or send an email to publisher@moontidepress.com.

Anonymous
Robin Axworthy
Conner Brenner
Bill Cushing
Susan Davis
Peggy Dobreer
Dennis Gowans
Half Off Books
Jim & Vicky Hoggatt
Ron Koertge & Bianca Richards
Ray & Christi Lacoste
Zachary & Tammy Locklin
David McIntire
José Enrique Medina
Michael Miller & Rachanee Srisavasdi
Terri Niccum
Ronny & Richard Morago
Jennifer Smith
Andrew Turner
Mariano Zaro

ALSO AVAILABLE FROM MOON TIDE PRESS

Lullaby of Teeth: An Anthology of Southern California Poetry (2017)
Angels in Seven, Michael Miller (2016)
A Likely Story, Robbie Nester (2014)
Embers on the Stairs, Ruth Bavetta (2014)
The Green of Sunset, John Brantingham (2013)
The Savagery of Bone, Timothy Matthew Perez (2013)
The Silence of Doorways, Sharon Venezio (2013)
Cosmos: An Anthology of Southern California Poetry (2012)
Straws and Shadows, Irena Praitis (2012)
In the Lake of Your Bones, Peggy Dobreer (2012)
I Was Building Up to Something, Susan Davis (2011)
Hopeless Cases, Michael Kramer (2011)
One World, Gail Newman (2011)
What We Ache For, Eric Morago (2010)
Now and Then, Lee Mallory (2009)
Pop Art: An Anthology of Southern California Poetry (2010)
In the Heaven of Never Before, Carine Topal (2008)
A Wild Region, Kate Buckley (2008)
Carving in Bone: An Anthology of Orange County Poetry (2007)
Kindness from a Dark God, Ben Trigg (2007)
A Thin Strands of Lights, Ricki Mandeville (2006)
Sleepyhead Assassins, Mindy Nettifee (2006)
Tide Pools: An Anthology of Orange County Poetry (2006)
Lost American Nights: Lyrics & Poems, Michael Ubaldini (2006)

www.ingramcontent.com/pod-product-compliance
Lightning Source LLC
Chambersburg PA
CBHW031204090426
42736CB00009B/784